EASY PIANO

Blues Standards

Visit Hal Leonard Online at
www.halleonard.com

ISBN 978-0-634-09260-2

7777 W. BLUEMOUND RD. P.O. BOX 13819 MILWAUKEE, WI 53213

Visit Hal Leonard Online at
www.halleonard.com

BORN UNDER A BAD SIGN

Words and Music by BOOKER T. JONES
and WILLIAM BELL

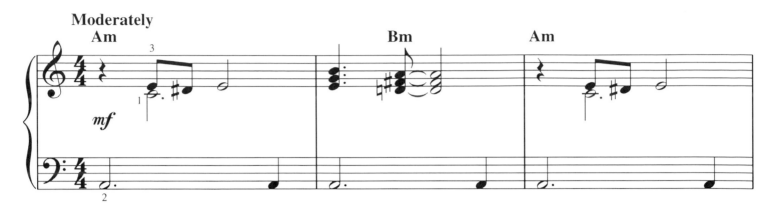

(See additional spoken lyrics 1)

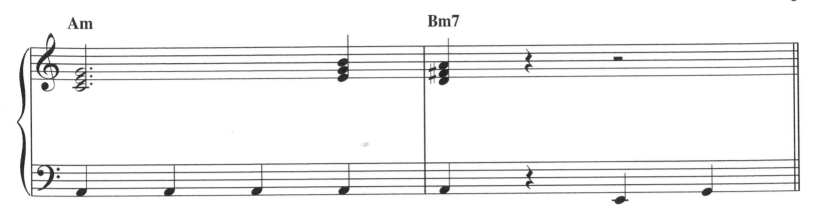

Born un-der a bad sign;

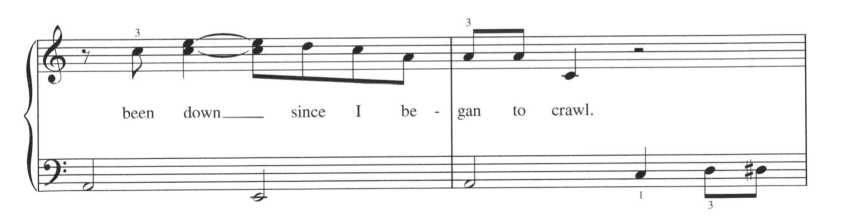

been down____ since I be - gan to crawl.

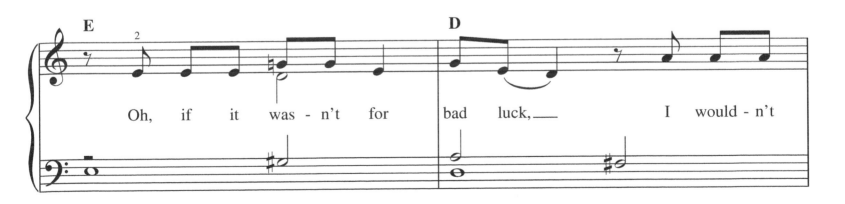

Oh, if it was-n't for bad luck,____ I would-n't

6

have no luck at all.   (Let___ me tell you.)

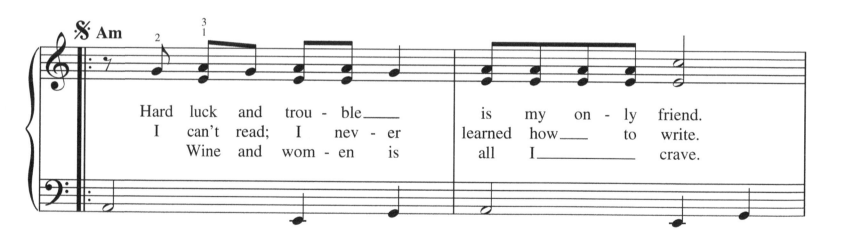

Hard luck and trou - ble___   is my on - ly friend.
I can't read; I nev - er   learned how___ to write.
Wine and wom - en is   all I_____ crave.

Been on my own___ ev - er   since I was ten.
My whole___ life___ has been   one big_____ fight.
A big head wom - an will car - ry   me to my grave.

Born un - der a bad sign;

been down____ since I be - gan to crawl.

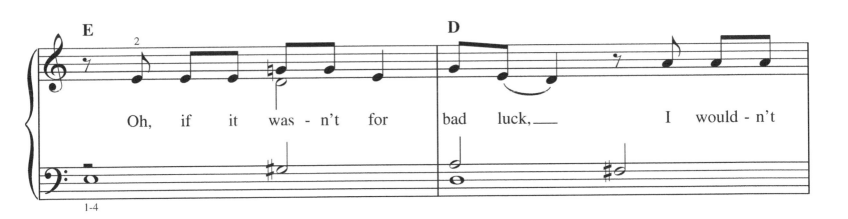

Oh, if it was - n't for bad luck,____ I would - n't

have no luck at all.

To Coda

(See additional spoken lyrics 2)

D.S. al Coda

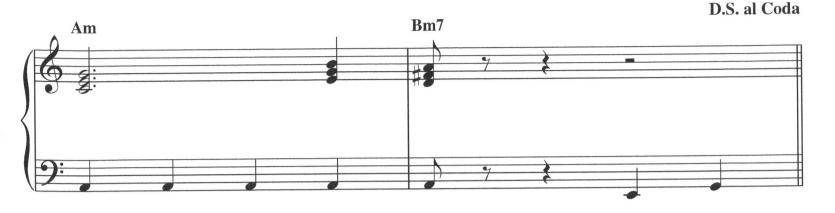

(See additional spoken lyrics 3)

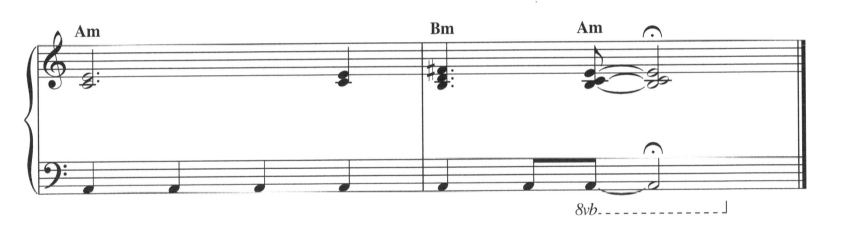

8vb

Additional Spoken Lyrics

1. When I was just a little boy, my daddy left home.
   He left my mama to go it all alone.
   You, know, the times were hard, but somehow we survived.
   Lord knows, it's a mystery to me how she managed to keep us alive.

2. I've often heard the old folks say, "Don't give up, when the chips are down,
   You got to keep on pushing." So I guess I gotta keep on pushing.
   You see, I was down, but I kind of picked myself up a little bit,
   Oh, and I had to dust myself off, clean myself up,
   And now, I'm gonna keep on pushing; I can't stop.

3. I'm gonna get myself together now, I'm gonna keep on pushing.

CALDONIA
(What Makes Your Big Head So Hard?)

Words and Music by
FLEECIE MOORE

Moderately fast Boogie-woogie

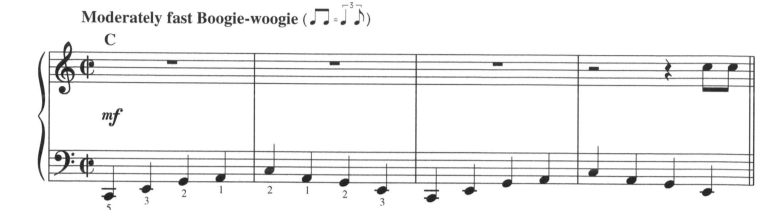

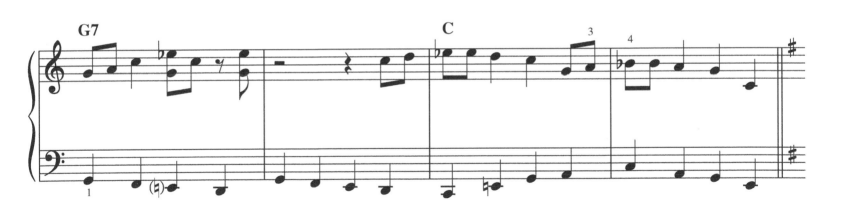

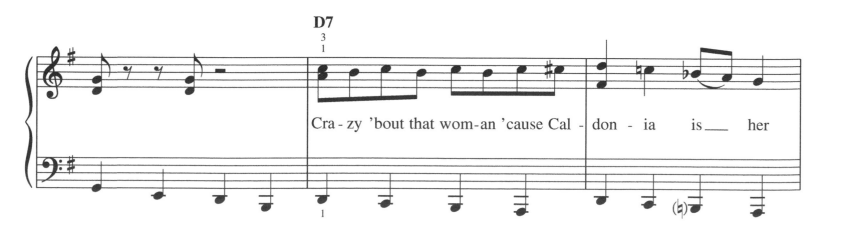

13

name. _____ Cal - don - ia! __ Cal -

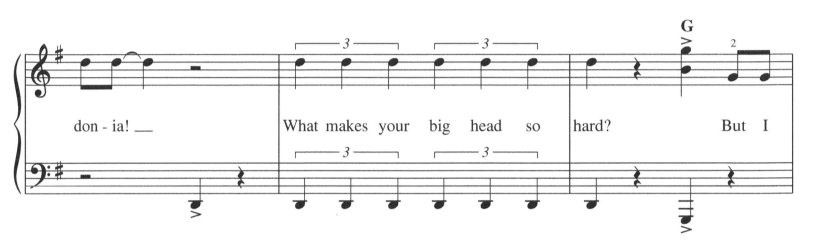

don - ia! __ What makes your big head so hard? But I

love you, love you just __ the same. _____

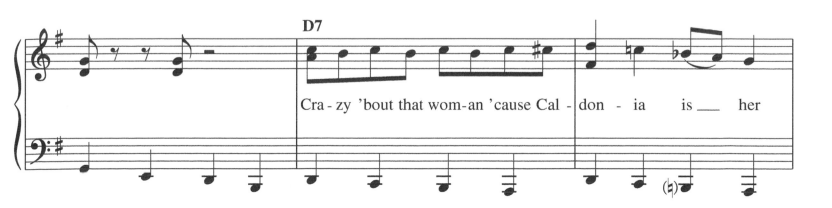

Cra - zy 'bout that wom-an 'cause Cal - don - ia is __ her

name.

(Spoken:) My mama told me to leave Caldonia alone;

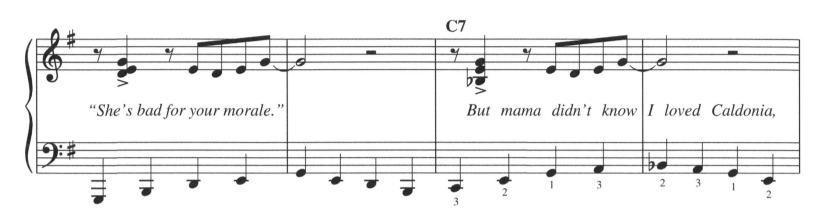

"She's bad for your morale." But mama didn't know I loved Caldonia,

she's such a swell gal! So I'm goin' down to Caldonia's house and ask her

just one more time. (Sung:) Cal- don-ia! __ Cal- don-ia! __

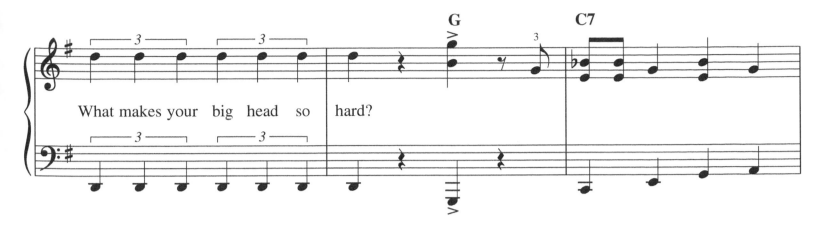

What makes your big head so hard?

EVERYDAY I HAVE THE BLUES

Words and Music by
PETER CHATMAN

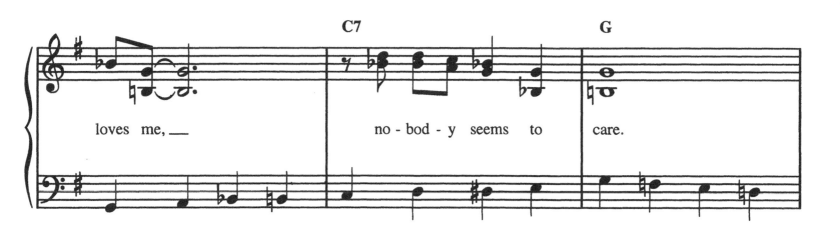

share. _____ _____ I'm gon-na pack my suit - case, _____ mov-in' on down the

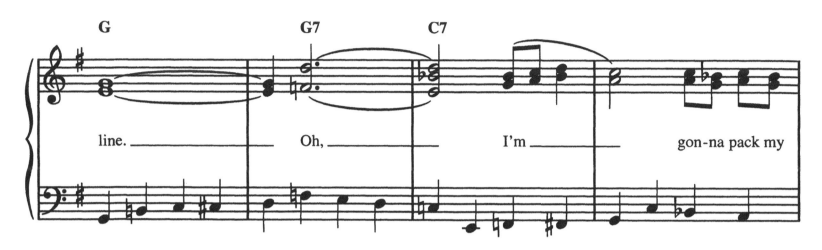

line. _____ Oh, _____ I'm _____ gon-na pack my

suit-case, move on down the line. Well, there ain't no - bod - y wor-ryin' and there

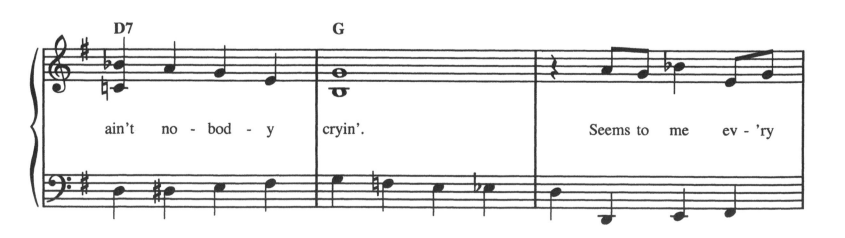

ain't no - bod - y cryin'. Seems to me ev - 'ry

day, ev - 'ry day, ev - 'ry day I have the blues.

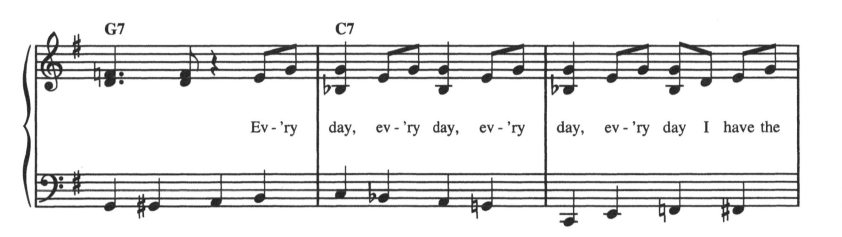

Ev - 'ry day, ev - 'ry day, ev - 'ry day, ev - 'ry day I have the

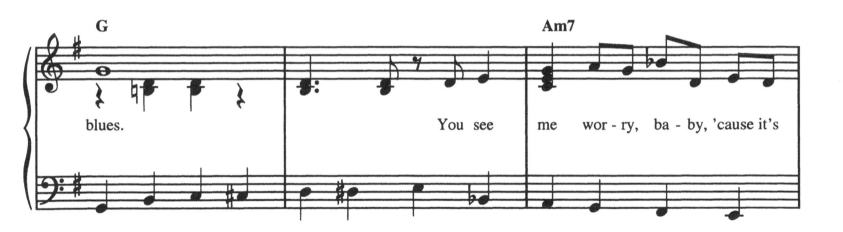

blues. You see me wor - ry, ba - by, 'cause it's

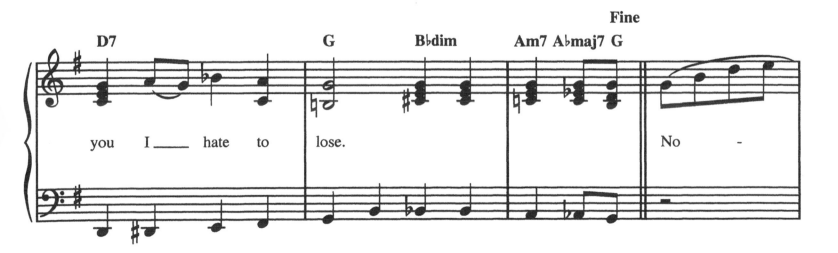

you I ___ hate to lose. No -

FURTHER ON UP THE ROAD

Words and Music by JOE VEASEY
and DON ROBEY

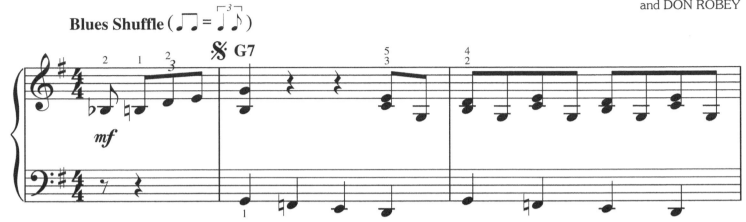

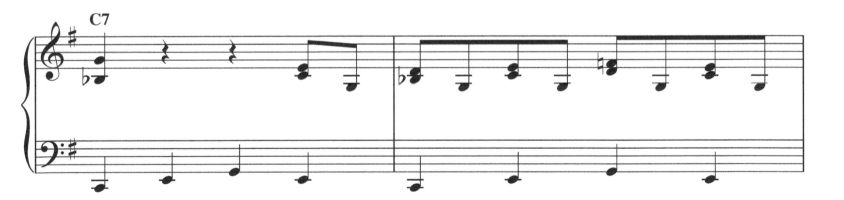

Fur - ther   on   up   the
Fur - ther   on   up   the

G7

road_____
road_____

some-bod-y's gon-na hurt you like you hurt me.
some-bod-y's gon-na hurt you like you hurt me.

C7

Fur-ther on up the road_____ some-bod-y's gon-na hurt you
Fur-ther on up the road_____ some-bod-y's gon-na hurt you,

G7 **D7**

like you hurt me._____ Fur-ther on up the road,
too. Fur-ther on up the road

C7 **G7** **To Coda** ⊕

ba-by, just you wait and see._____
some-bod-y's gon-na hurt you, too._____

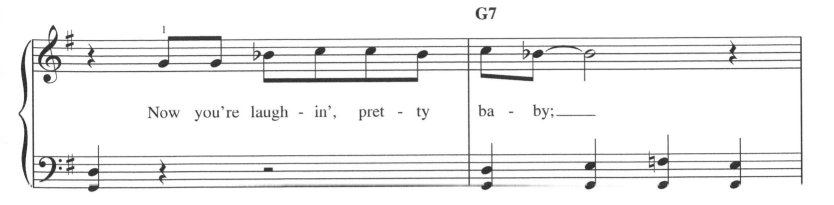

Now you're laugh - in', pret - ty ba - by;____

pret - ty soon you're gon - na be cry - in'.____

Now you're laugh - in', pret - ty ba - by;____

pret - ty soon you're gon - na be cry - in'.____

D7 **C7**

Fur-ther on up the road, you'll find out I was-n't

G7

D.S. al Coda

ly - in'._____

CODA

Fur-ther on up the road. Fur-ther on up the

G7

road._____ Fur - ther on_____ up the

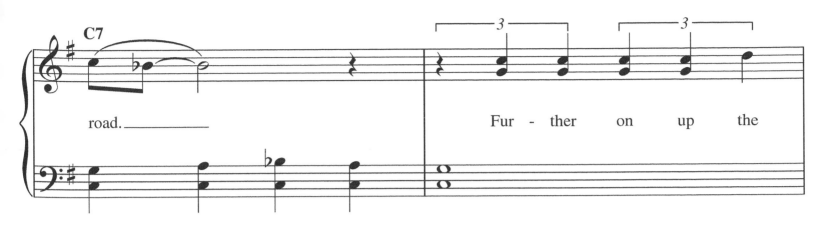

road. _____

Fur - ther on up the

road.

Fur - ther on up the

road

you're gon - na find out I was - n't ly -

in'.

HOW LONG, HOW LONG BLUES

Words and Music by
LEROY CARR

train.   Way down in   my ____ heart I had an ach - in'

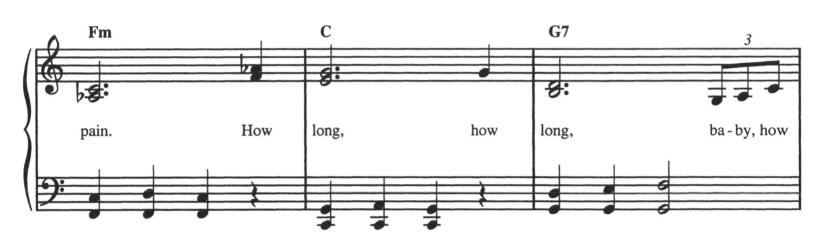

pain.   How   long,   how   long,   ba - by, how

long?   I'm sad and lone - ly   all the whole . day

through.   Why don't you   write me   and give me the

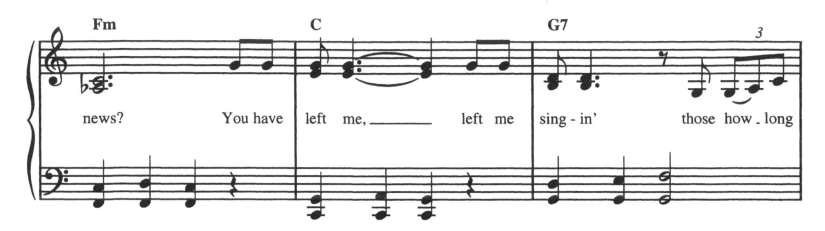

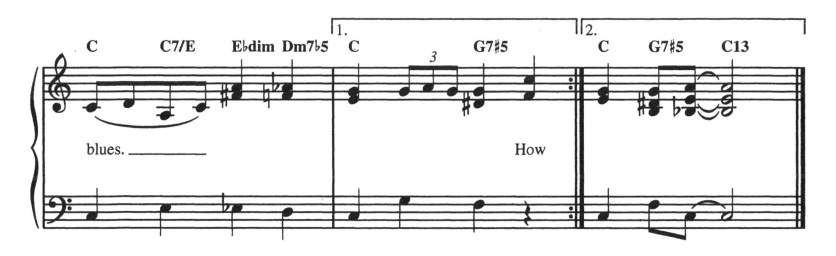

Additional lyrics (ad lib.)

If I could holler like a Mountain Jack,
I'd go up on the mountain and call my baby back,
How long, how long, how long.

I went up on the mountain looked as far as I could see,
The $\left(\begin{array}{c}\text{man}\\\text{woman}\end{array}\right)$ had my $\left(\begin{array}{c}\text{woman}\\\text{man}\end{array}\right)$ and the blues had poor me,
How long, how long, how long.

I can see the green grass growing on the hill,
But I ain't seen the green grass on a dollar bill,
For so long, so long, baby, so long.

If you don't believe I'm sinkin' see what a hole I'm in,
If you don't believe me, baby, look what a fool I've been,
Well, I'm gone how long, baby, how long.

I'm goin' down to Georgia, been up in Tennessee,
So look me over, baby, the last you'll see of me,
For so long, so long, baby, so long.

The brook runs into the river, the river runs into the sea.
If I don't run into my baby, a train is goin' to run into me,
How long, how long, how long.

I'M YOUR HOOCHIE COOCHIE MAN

Written by WILLIE DIXON

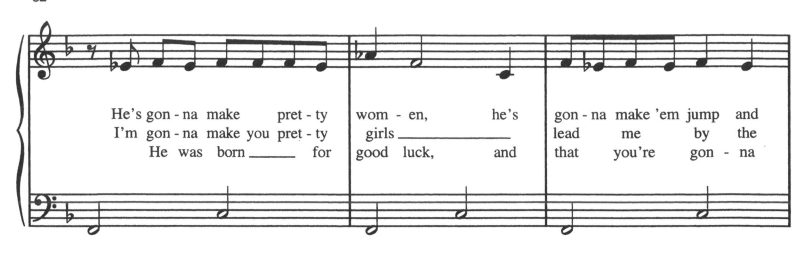

He's gon - na make pret - ty wom - en, he's gon - na make 'em jump and
I'm gon - na make you pret - ty girls _____ lead me by the
He was born _____ for good luck, and that you're gon - na

shout.
hand. Then the world could know
see. Then the world will know
I've got sev - en hun - dred dol - lars, ba - by,

B♭7

what this was all a - bout.
I'm the hoo - chie coo - chie man. Lord, _ I'm here, ___
don't you mess with me.

oh yeah. Ev - 'ry - bod - y knows _ I'm

here, ___ oh Lord, ___ 'cause I'm a

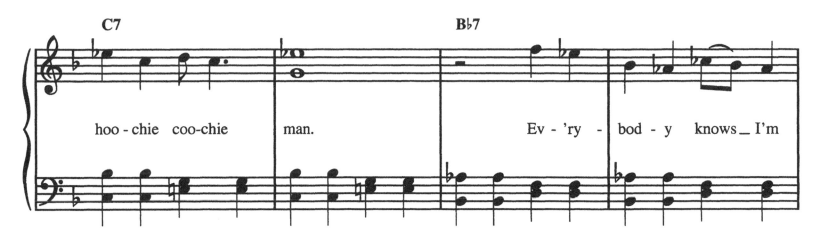

hoo - chie coo-chie man. Ev - 'ry - bod - y knows ___ I'm

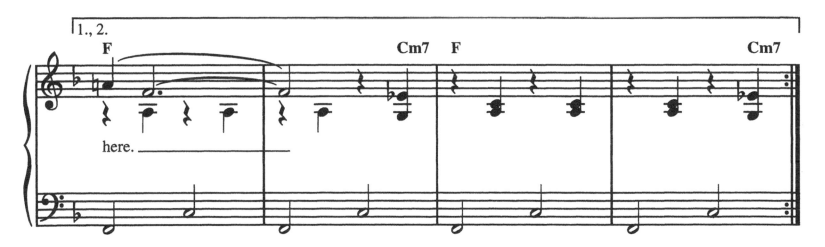

1., 2.

here. _____

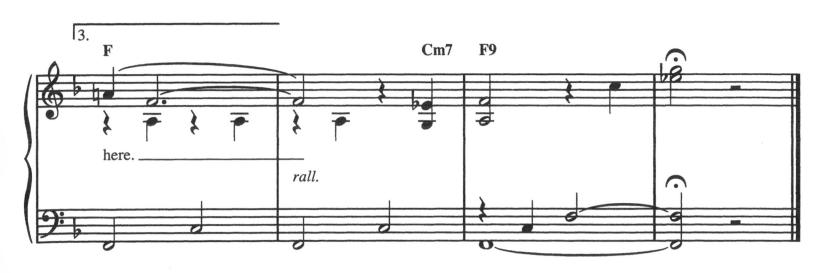

3.

here. _____

rall.

IT HURTS ME TOO

Words and Music by
MEL LONDON

C

more,_____ when you should love him less, why sneak up be -

F7　　　　　　　　　　　　　　　　　　　　**F#dim**

hind him_____ and you take this mess. When things go

C/G　　　　　　**Am**　　　　　　　　**G**

wrong,　　　　　　go wrong with you,　　　　　it hurts me

C　　**C7**　　**F**　　**A♭/G♭**　　**C/G**　　**G7#5**

too.　　　　　　　　　　　　　　He loves an - oth - er

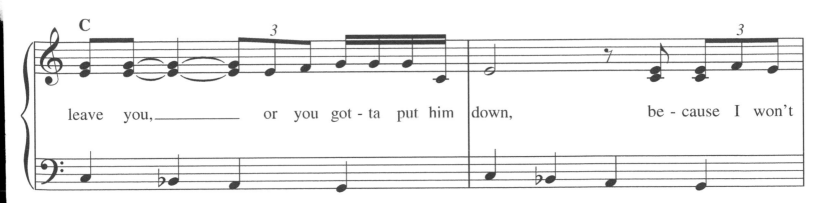

leave you,_____ or you got-ta put him down, be - cause I won't

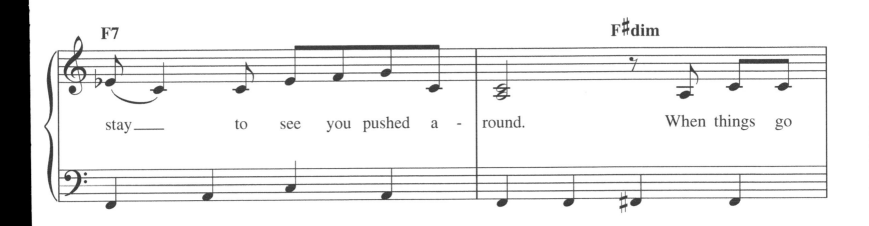

stay___ to see you pushed a - round. When things go

wrong, go wrong with you, it hurts me

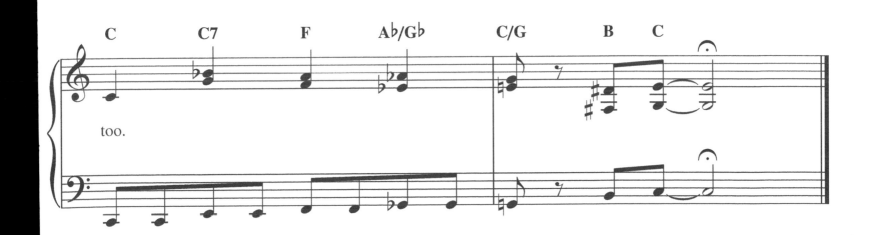

too.

MY BABE

Written by WILLIE DIXON

Medium beat

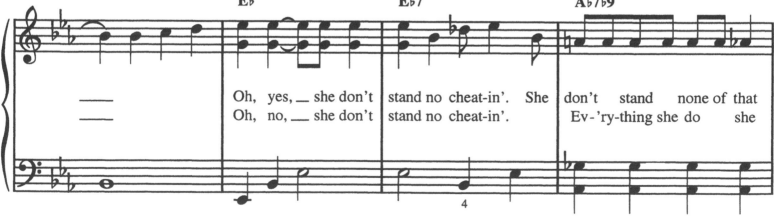

My babe, ___ she don't stand no cheat - in', my babe. ___
My babe, ___ she don't stand no cheat - in', my babe. ___

___
Oh, yes, ___ she don't stand no cheat - in', my babe. ___
My, babe, ___ she don't stand no cheat - in', my babe. ___

___
Oh, yes, ___ she don't stand no cheat-in'. She don't stand none of that
Oh, no, ___ she don't stand no cheat-in'. Ev-'ry-thing she do she

4

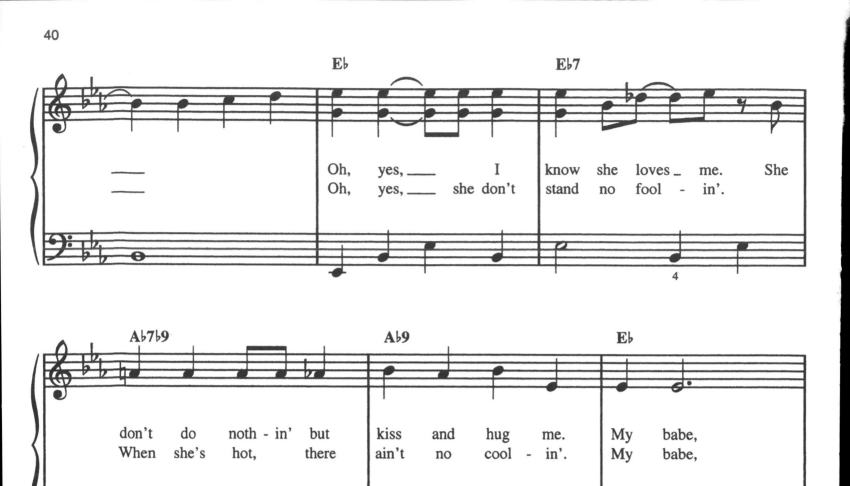

Oh, yes, ___ I know she loves ___ me. She
Oh, yes, ___ she don't stand no fool - in'.

don't do noth - in' but kiss and hug me. My babe,
When she's hot, there ain't no cool - in'. My babe,

1.
true lit - tle ba - by is my babe.
true lit - tle ba - by is

Repeat and Fade

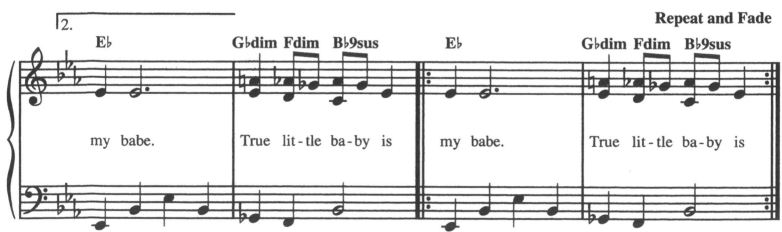

2.
my babe. True lit - tle ba - by is my babe. True lit - tle ba - by is

ROUTE 66

By BOBBY TROUP

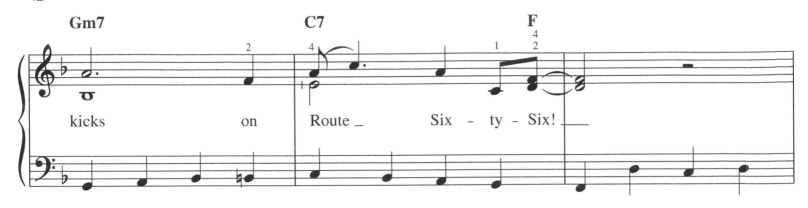

kicks   on   Route _   Six - ty - Six! _

It   winds _____ from Chi - ca - go   to   L. A.

_   more than   two _____ thou-sand

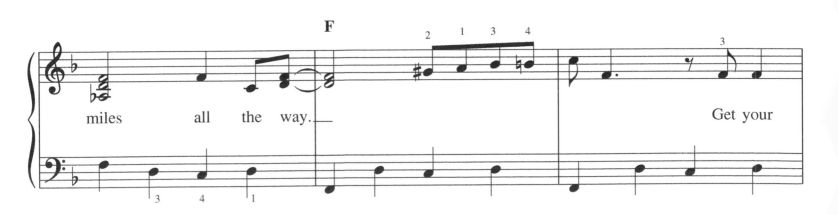

miles   all   the way. _   Get your

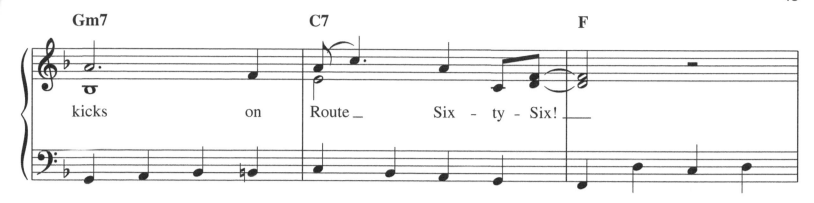

kicks   on   Route — Six - ty - Six! —

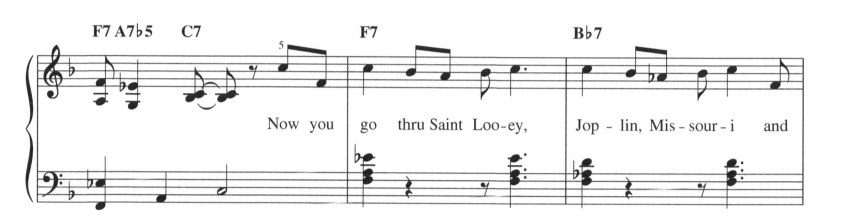

Now you go   thru Saint Loo-ey,   Jop - lin, Mis - sour - i   and

Ok - la - hom - a Cit - y is might   -   y pret - ty. You'll see —

—   Am - ar - il - lo, —   Gal - lup, New

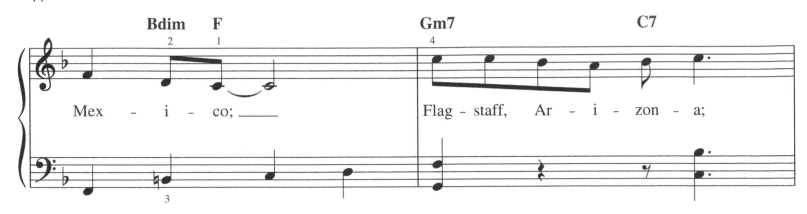

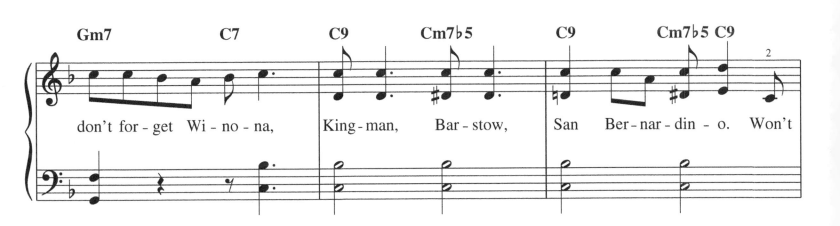

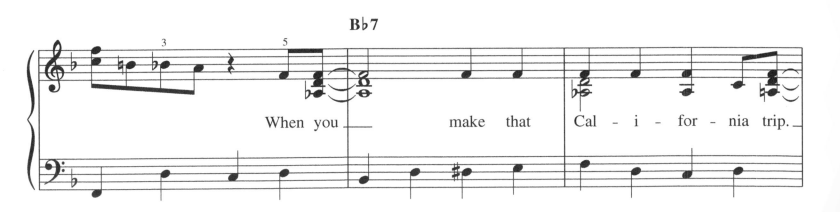

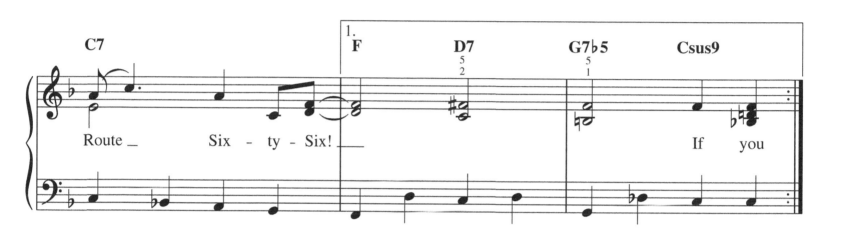

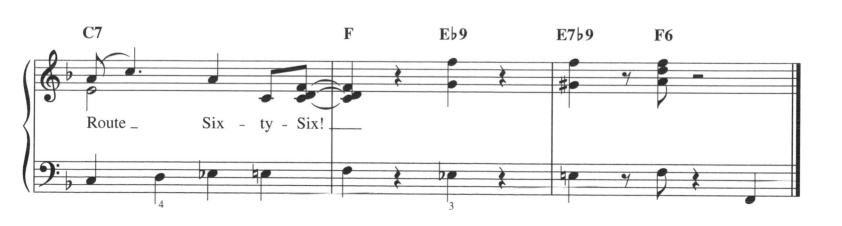

NOBODY KNOWS YOU WHEN YOU'RE DOWN AND OUT

Words and Music by
JIMMIE COX

bought boot - leg whis - key. ___ cham-pagne and

wine. ___ Then I be - gan ___ to fall so

low. Lost all my good friends; ___

I did not have no - where to go. I get my

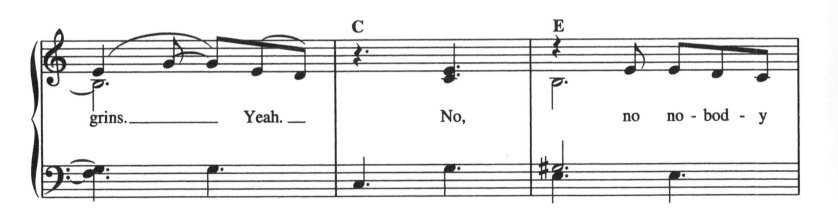

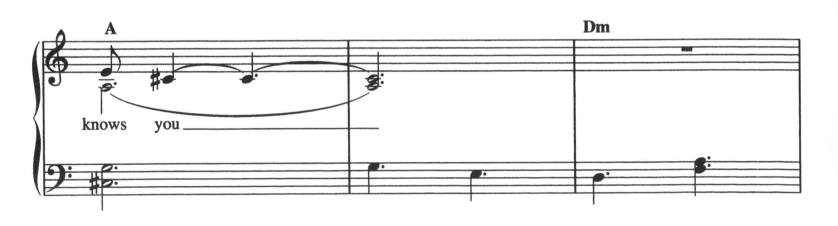

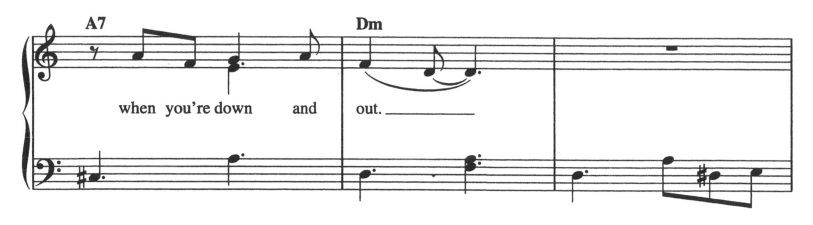

when you're down and out. _____

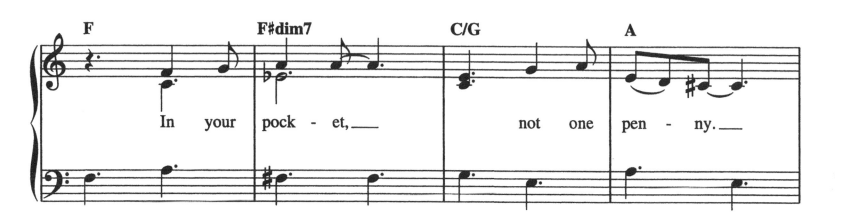

In your pock - et, ____ not one pen - ny. ____

And as for friends, you don't have

an - y. ____ When you fi - n'lly get back up on your

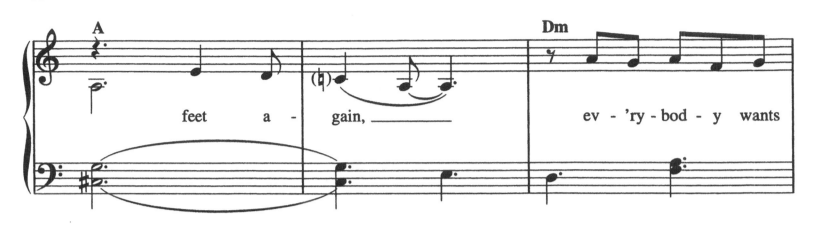

51

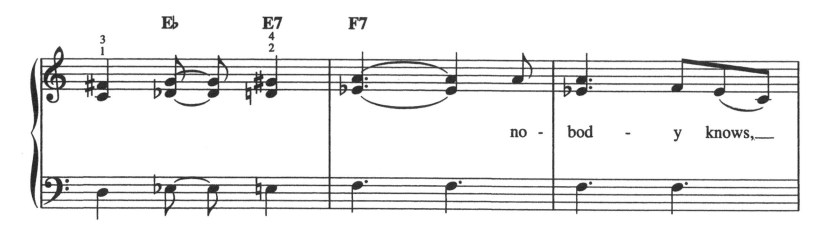

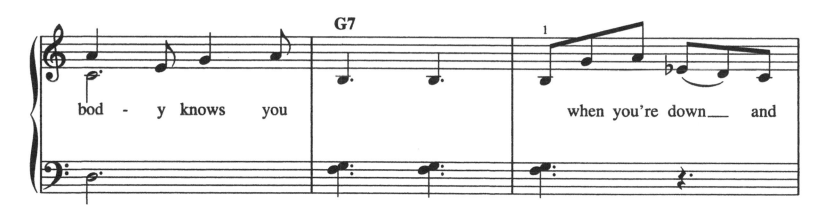

PLEASE ACCEPT MY LOVE

Words and Music by B.B. KING
and SAUL BIHARI

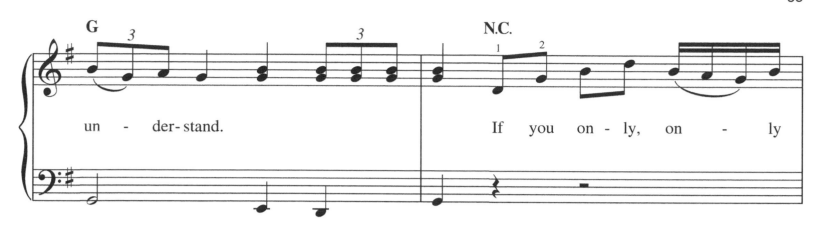

un - der-stand.   If you on - ly, on - ly

knew   just how much I_____ love you.

Lov-ing you   the way that I do,_____   you'd take to-night to

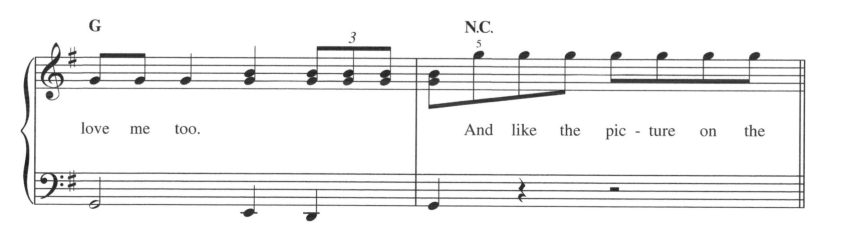

love me too.   And like the pic - ture on the

ROCK ME BABY

Words and Music by B.B. KING
and JOE BIHARI

Rock me, ba - by,   rock me   all __ night   long. _____
Rock me, ba - by,   like you   roll __ a   wa - gon wheel. _
Rock me, ba - by,   hon - ey   rock _ me   slow. _____

SEE SEE RIDER

Words and Music by
MA RAINEY

(They Call It)
STORMY MONDAY
(Stormy Monday Blues)

Words and Music by
AARON "T-BONE" WALKER

Slow, Dirty Blues

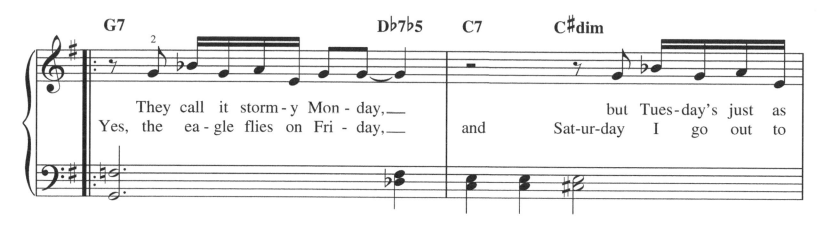

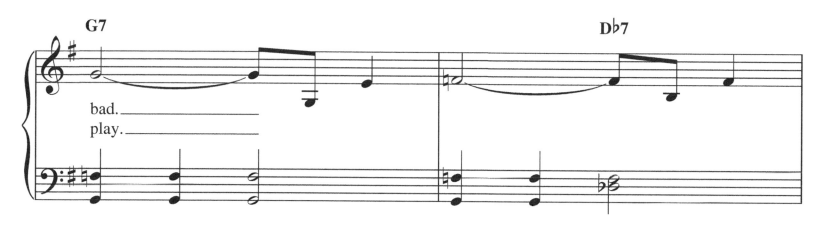

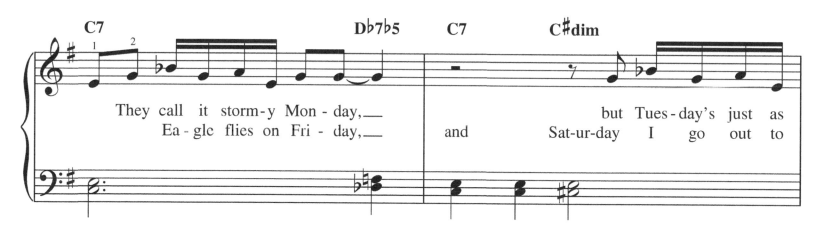

and Thurs-day's al - so sad.
then I kneel down to pray.

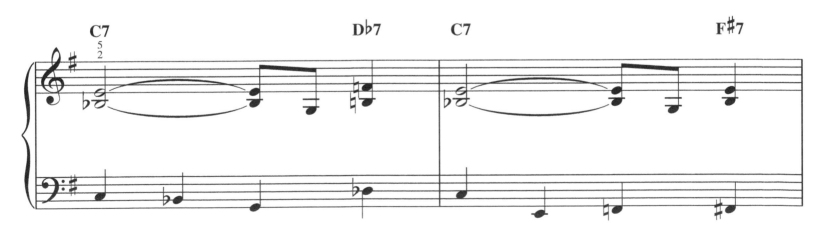

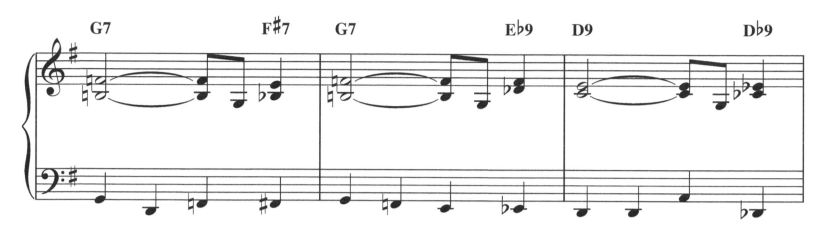

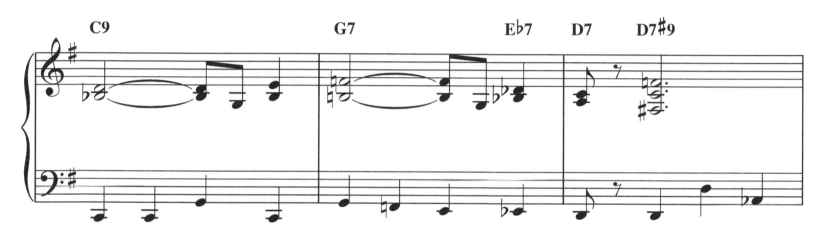

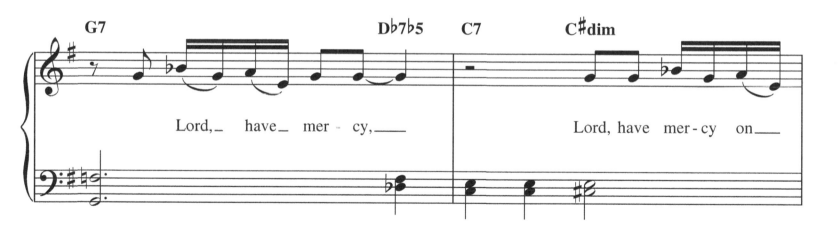

Lord,_ have_ mer - cy,____ Lord, have mer - cy on____

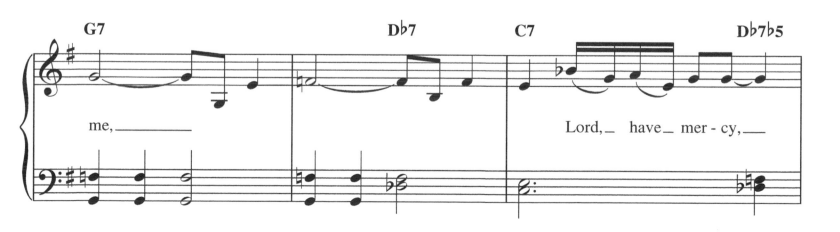

me,_____ Lord,_ have_ mer - cy,____

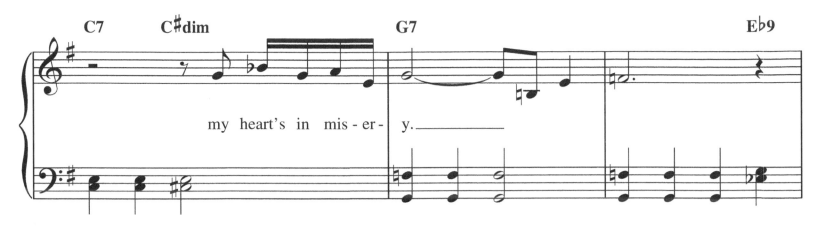

my heart's in mis - er - y. _____

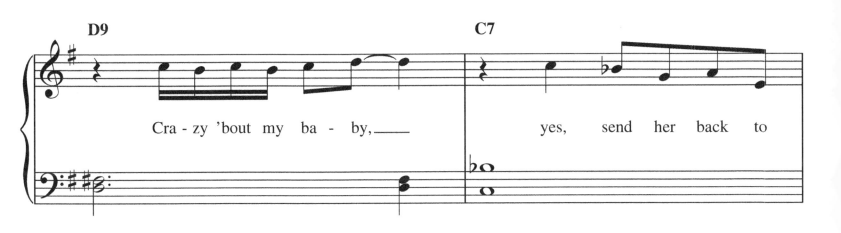

Cra - zy 'bout my ba - by, _____ yes, send her back to

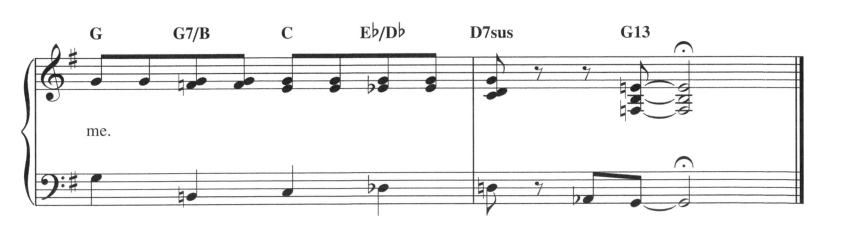

me.

THREE O'CLOCK BLUES

Words and Music by B.B. KING
and JULES BIHARI

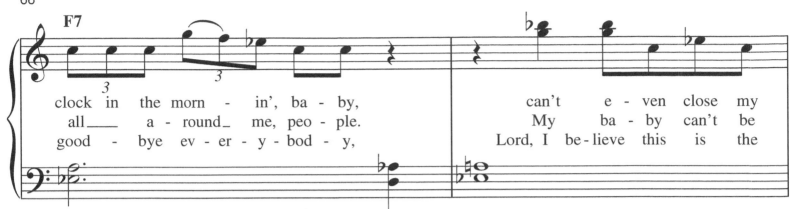

clock in the morn - in', baby, | can't e - ven close my
all___ a - round___ me, peo - ple. | My ba - by can't be
good - bye ev - er - y - bod - y, | Lord, I be - lieve this is the

eyes. | Well, I
found. | Well, if
end. | Well,___

can't find my ba - by. | Lord, and I can't be sat - is -
I don't find my ba - by, | I'm go - in' down to the bowl - in'
you can tell my ba - by | to___ for - give me for my

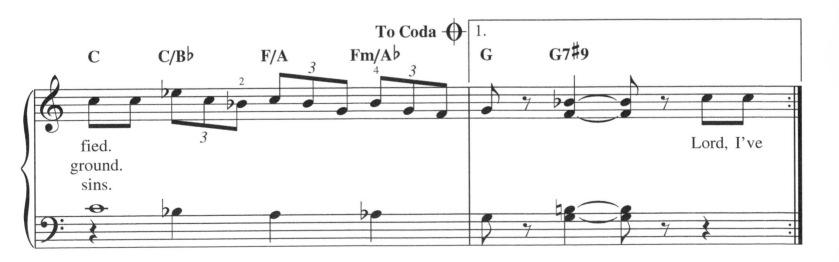

fied. | Lord, I've
ground.
sins.

SWEET HOME CHICAGO

Words and Music by
ROBERT JOHNSON

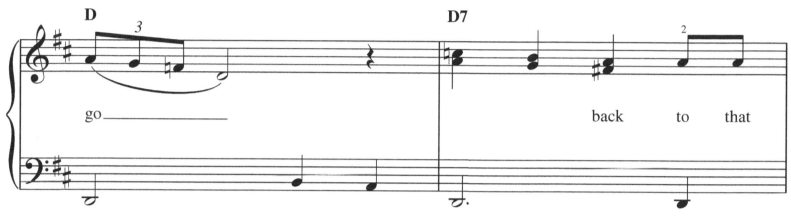

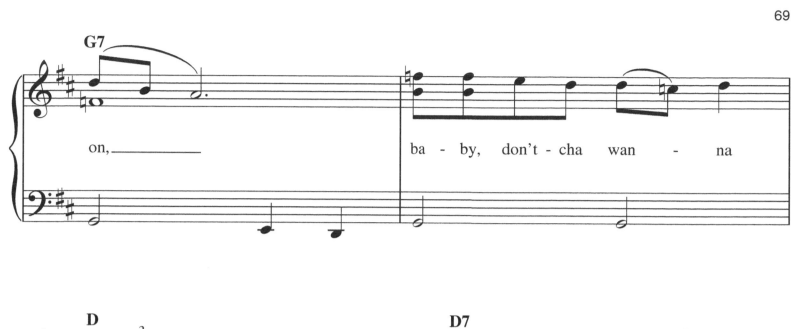

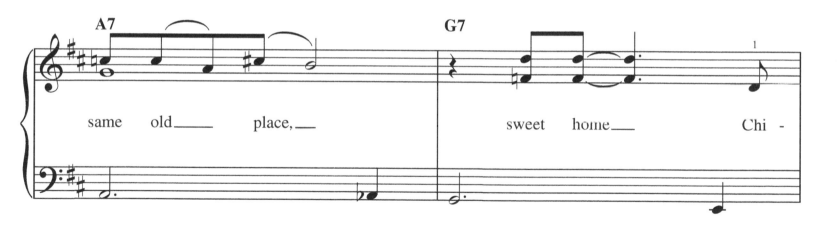

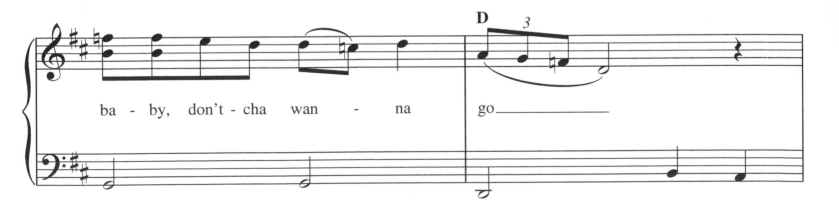

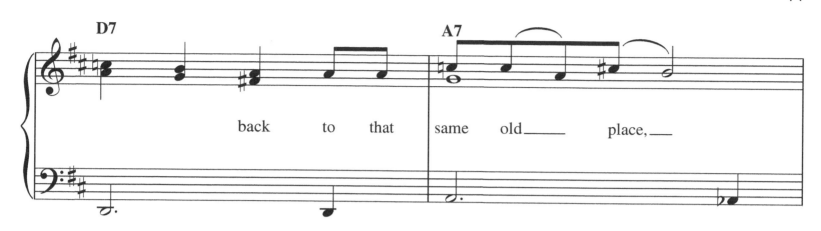

back to that same old___ place,___

To Coda ⊕

D.S. al Coda
(take 2nd ending)

sweet home__ Chi - ca - go.___ Come

CODA ⊕

Come on,___ ba - by, don't-cha wan - na

go.___ Come on,___

TEXAS FLOOD

Words and Music by LARRY DAVIS
and JOSEPH W. SCOTT

Bb7

Tex - as, _____ and all the tel - e - phone lines are
roll - ing; man, I'm stand-ing out here in the
ba - by. Lord, I'm go - ing back home to

F7

down. Well, I been
rain. Well,
stay. Well, where there's

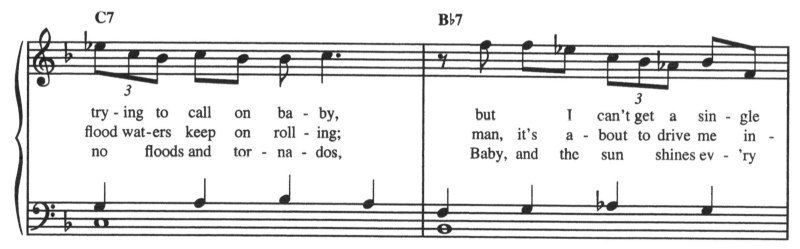

C7   **Bb7**

try - ing to call on ba - by, but I can't get a sin - gle
flood wat-ers keep on roll - ing; man, it's a - bout to drive me in -
no floods and tor - na - dos, Baby, and the sun shines ev - 'ry

F   1.,2. **Gm7**   **C7**   3. **C7#5 F**

sound.
sane. Well,
day. Well,

THE THRILL IS GONE

Words and Music by ROY HAWKINS
and RICK DARNELL

KEYBOARD STYLE SERIES

THE COMPLETE GUIDE!

These book/audio packs provide focused lessons that contain valuable how-to insight, essential playing tips, and beneficial information for all players. From comping to soloing, comprehensive treatment is given to each subject. The companion audio features many of the examples in the book performed either solo or with a full band.

BEBOP JAZZ PIANO
by John Valerio

This book provides detailed information for bebop and jazz keyboardists on: chords and voicings, harmony and chord progressions, scales and tonality, common melodic figures and patterns, comping, characteristic tunes, the styles of Bud Powell and Thelonious Monk, and more.
00290535 Book/Online Audio $18.99

BEGINNING ROCK KEYBOARD
by Mark Harrison

This comprehensive book/audio package will teach you the basic skills needed to play beginning rock keyboard. From comping to soloing, you'll learn the theory, the tools, and the techniques used by the pros. The accompanying audio demonstrates most of the music examples in the book.
00311922 Book/Online Audio $14.99

BLUES PIANO
by Mark Harrison

With this book/audio pack, you'll learn the theory, the tools, and even the tricks that the pros use to play the blues. Covers: scales and chords; left-hand patterns; walking bass; endings and turnarounds; right-hand techniques; how to solo with blues scales; crossover licks; and more.
00311007 Book/Online Audio $19.99

BOOGIE-WOOGIE PIANO
by Todd Lowry

From learning the basic chord progressions to inventing your own melodic riffs, you'll learn the theory, tools and techniques used by the genre's best practicioners.
00117067 Book/Online Audio $17.99

BRAZILIAN PIANO
by Robert Willey and Alfredo Cardim

Brazilian Piano teaches elements of some of the most appealing Brazilian musical styles: choro, samba, and bossa nova. It starts with rhythmic training to develop the fundamental groove of Brazilian music.
00311469 Book/Online Audio $19.99

CONTEMPORARY JAZZ PIANO
by Mark Harrison

From comping to soloing, you'll learn the theory, the tools, and the techniques used by the pros. The full band tracks on the audio feature the rhythm section on the left channel and the piano on the right channel, so that you can play along with the band.
00311848 Book/Online Audio $18.99

COUNTRY PIANO
by Mark Harrison

Learn the theory, the tools, and the tricks used by the pros to get that authentic country sound. This book/audio pack covers: scales and chords, walkup and walkdown patterns, comping in traditional and modern country, Nashville "fretted piano" techniques and more.
00311052 Book/Online Audio $19.99

GOSPEL PIANO
by Kurt Cowling

Discover the tools you need to play in a variety of authentic gospel styles, through a study of rhythmic devices, grooves, melodic and harmonic techniques, and formal design. The accompanying audio features over 90 tracks, including piano examples as well as the full gospel band.
00311327 Book/Online Adio $17.99

INTRO TO JAZZ PIANO
by Mark Harrison

From comping to soloing, you'll learn the theory, the tools, and the techniques used by the pros. The accompanying audio demonstrates most of the music examples in the book. The full band tracks feature the rhythm section on the left channel and the piano on the right channel, so that you can play along with the band.
00312088 Book/Online Audio $17.99

JAZZ-BLUES PIANO
by Mark Harrison

This comprehensive book will teach you the basic skills needed to play jazz-blues piano. Topics covered include: scales and chords • harmony and voicings • progressions and comping • melodies and soloing • characteristic stylings.
00311243 Book/Online Audio $17.99

JAZZ-ROCK KEYBOARD
by T. Lavitz

Learn what goes into mixing the power and drive of rock music with the artistic elements of jazz improvisation in this comprehensive book and CD package. This instructional tool delves into scales and modes, and how they can be used with various chord progressions to develop the best in soloing chops.
00290536 Book/CD Pack..........$17.95

LATIN JAZZ PIANO
by John Valerio

This book is divided into three sections. The first covers Afro-Cuban (Afro-Caribbean) jazz, the second section deals with Brazilian influenced jazz – Bossa Nova and Samba, and the third contains lead sheets of the tunes and instructions for the play-along audio.
00311345 Book/Online Audio $17.99

MODERN POP KEYBOARD
by Mark Harrison

From chordal comping to arpeggios and ostinatos, from grand piano to synth pads, you'll learn the theory, the tools, and the techniques used by the pros. The online audio demonstrates most of the music examples in the book.
00146596 Book/Online Audio $17.99

NEW AGE PIANO
by Todd Lowry

From melodic development to chord progressions to left-hand accompaniment patterns, you'll learn the theory, the tools and the techniques used by the pros. The accompanying 96-track CD demonstrates most of the music examples in the book.
00117322 Book/CD Pack..........$16.99

POST-BOP JAZZ PIANO
by John Valerio

This book/audio pack will teach you the basic skills needed to play post-bop jazz piano. Learn the theory, the tools, and the tricks used by the pros to play in the style of Bill Evans, Thelonious Monk, Herbie Hancock, McCoy Tyner, Chick Corea and others. Topics covered include: chord voicings, scales and tonality, modality, and more.
00311005 Book/Online Audio $17.99

PROGRESSIVE ROCK KEYBOARD
by Dan Maske

You'll learn how soloing techniques, form, rhythmic and metrical devices, harmony, and counterpoint all come together to make this style of rock the unique and exciting genre it is.
00311307 Book/Online Audio $19.99

R&B KEYBOARD
by Mark Harrison

From soul to funk to disco to pop, you'll learn the theory, the tools, and the tricks used by the pros with this book/audio pack. Topics covered include: scales and chords, harmony and voicings, progressions and comping, rhythmic concepts, characteristic stylings, the development of R&B, and more! Includes seven songs.
00310881 Book/Online Audio $19.99

ROCK KEYBOARD
by Scott Miller

Learn to comp or solo in any of your favorite rock styles. Listen to the audio to hear your parts fit in with the total groove of the band. Includes 99 tracks! Covers: classic rock, pop/rock, blues rock, Southern rock, hard rock, progressive rock, alternative rock and heavy metal.
00310823 Book/Online Audio $17.99

ROCK 'N' ROLL PIANO
by Andy Vinter

Take your place alongside Fats Domino, Jerry Lee Lewis, Little Richard, and other legendary players of the '50s and '60s! This book/audio pack covers: left-hand patterns; basic rock 'n' roll progressions; right-hand techniques; straight eighths vs. swing eighths; glisses, crushed notes, rolls, note clusters and more. Includes six complete tunes.
00310912 Book/Online Audio $18.99

SALSA PIANO
by Hector Martignon

From traditional Cuban music to the more modern Puerto Rican and New York styles, you'll learn the all-important rhythmic patterns of salsa and how to apply them to the piano. The book provides historical, geographical and cultural background info, and the 50+-tracks includes piano examples and a full salsa band percussion section.
00311049 Book/Online Audio $19.99

SMOOTH JAZZ PIANO
by Mark Harrison

Learn the skills you need to play smooth jazz piano – the theory, the tools, and the tricks used by the pros. Topics covered include: scales and chords; harmony and voicings; progressions and comping; rhythmic concepts; melodies and soloing; characteristic stylings; discussions on jazz evolution.
00311095 Book/Online Audio $19.99

STRIDE & SWING PIANO
by John Valerio

Learn the styles of the stride and swing piano masters, such as Scott Joplin, Jimmy Yancey, Pete Johnson, Jelly Roll Morton, James P. Johnson, Fats Waller, Teddy Wilson, and Art Tatum. This book/audio pack covers classic ragtime, early blues and boogie woogie, New Orleans jazz and more. Includes 14 songs.
00310882 Book/Online Audio $19.99

WORSHIP PIANO
by Bob Kauflin

From chord inversions to color tones, from rhythmic patterns to the Nashville Numbering System, you'll learn the tools and techniques needed to play piano or keyboard in a modern worship setting.
00311425 Book/Online Audio $17.99

HAL•LEONARD®

Prices, contents, and availability subject to change without notice.

www.halleonard.com